Guide to the
New
Testament

Harold Shaw Publishers
Wheaton, Illinois

Cover photo: V. Gilbert Beers
New Testament site of Ephesus theater

First printing, February 1990

INTRODUCTION

In the Old Testament, God promised Israel that someday he would make a new covenant (or testament) with his people (Jeremiah 31:31-34). At that time he would "write the law upon their hearts" instead of on stone tablets (like the Ten Commandments). Jesus established that "new testament" with his life, death, and resurrection, and therefore the writings that relate to him and his church are called the *New Testament*. It has four sections: the Gospels, Acts, the Epistles (or letters), and Revelation.

The Gospels

The first section of the New Testament, called the Gospels, consists of four accounts of the life of Jesus. (The word *gospel* means "good news.") The first three gospels have been given the title "synoptic" because they look at Jesus' life from a similar point of view.

Acts

The second section of the New Testament is one book, the Book of Acts. It contains the history of the early church from Jesus' ascension to the imprisonment of the apostle Paul in Rome. In Acts we have the story of the gospel going from Jerusalem to Judea to Samaria and then out to the distant parts of the earth (Acts 1:8). Even today, Christians are called to continue that story of concern for the world and evangelistic outreach.

The Epistles (Letters)

The third section of the New Testament contains the letters of apostolic writers. The largest number were written by the apostle Paul (Romans—Philemon). His writings have been subgrouped into letters (Romans, 1 and 2 Corinthians, Galatians, 1 and 2 Thessalonians); prison letters (Ephesians, Philippians, Colossians, Philemon); and pastoral letters (1 and 2 Timothy, Titus). Hebrews is considered by some scholars to have been written by Paul as well. The remaining letters, James—Jude, are called general or *catholic* letters because most of them except 2 and 3 John, were written to the church at large (generally) as opposed to individual churches or people.

Revelation

The fourth section of the New Testament consists of one book, Revelation, which is also called the Apocalypse. It stands by itself as a book of prophecy depicting the eventual course of history, both on earth and beyond this life. Here we find a picture of heaven and the promise of being forever with the Lord.

THE GOSPELS

Matthew
Author: Matthew
Date: between A.D. 60 & A.D. 80

Content

The Gospel of Matthew has been one of the favorite books of the church throughout its history for several reasons. It is the most detailed regarding Jesus' life; it contains the famous "Sermon on the Mount," a collection of teaching that even nonbelievers hold in high regard; it is richest in detail about the birth of Jesus, a traditionally interesting event because of our celebration of Christmas; and it includes a large collection of parables for which Jesus is remembered as a master teacher.

Opinion differs as to when this Gospel was written. Those who put it earlier (c. A.D. 60) point to Jesus' predictions about the destruction of Jerusalem (which took place in A.D. 70) and argue that they are regarded as future. Those who make it later (c. A.D. 80) say it has all the appearance of being a later document, reflecting a more developed situation. The book has no author's name attached to it, but very early in its history Matthew was regarded as the author and there is no reason to doubt that this is true.

The Gospel of Matthew was written for a number of reasons, some practical, some theological. Practically, there was a need for more information about Jesus. As people were becoming believers, questions were being asked that needed answers. It simply wasn't possible to travel to Jerusalem and ask the apostles, but a book dealing with the basic facts could be sent to each congregation. There was also a need for accurate information. Jesus' enemies were spreading lies about him. Others, who were trying to get personal gain from the new movement, were altering the facts to suit their own purposes. Followers of Jesus, like Matthew, wanted to set the record straight. The death of some of the apostles also made it necessary to put this valuable material in writing. If all those who knew Jesus were gone, who would be around to tell the story? Had Matthew (and the other three Gospel writers) not done this, Christianity might never have been more than a local, ancient phenomenon. God had a hand in this documentation, guiding selected people to preserve the truth for future generations. So the Book of Matthew functioned as something of a handbook for believers.

Theological Themes

Matthew had other reasons to write than just the practical needs of the church. He was trying to confront some special problems and to stress particular things in his writing. First, he realized the importance of Old Testament prophecy and how it was fulfilled in Jesus' life. The church did not arise by accident, nor was it unplanned for by God. Throughout the whole Old Testament the days that had now arrived had been predicted. Matthew showed how virtually all the events of Jesus' life were foreseen by the prophets: his birth, events surrounding his early life, healings, teachings, arrest, death, and resurrection.

Second, Matthew was concerned to show to his Jewish readers that Jesus was the fulfillment of their history and dreams. He was, in fact, the Messiah who was to come. The very first verse of the book shows this: Jesus was "the son of David, the son of Abraham."

Third, Matthew was concerned to show that although Jesus came *from* the Jews, he came *for* all people, Gentiles included. Consequently, emphasis is placed on the coming of the Magi (Wise Men) to acknowledge Jesus' birth, the inclusion of the Gentiles in the kingdom, and the command to go into all the world to preach the gospel to every creature.

Fourth, Matthew specifically mentioned the founding of the church and how certain problems should be handled.

Finally, Jesus' teachings are prominent in Matthew's gospel as a guide for believers. Large sections are devoted to what Jesus said about basic circumstances of life (5:3–7:27; 10:5-42; 13:3-52; 18:3-35; 24:4–25:46).

Geographical Features of Palestine

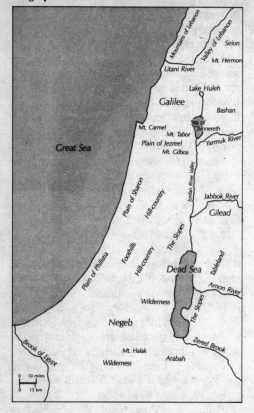

Outline

Mark

Author: Mark
Date: c. A.D. 60

Content

The Gospel of Mark was probably the first gospel written, forming the base, in one way or another, for both Matthew and Luke. The three together are called "Synoptics" because they view the life of Jesus from roughly the same angle. The Gospel of John takes a different tack, and hence it is usually discussed by itself. Mark has all the appearances of being written early in the church's history, certainly before the fall of Jerusalem in A.D. 70.

There are two basic theories regarding authorship. A modern view suggests that the book arose over a period of time, being added to, edited, altered, and rearranged according to the current needs of the church. Although some passages in this Gospel look as though they have been reworked, such a wholesale revamping is unlikely. The church would hardly have felt it right to alter the life of Jesus so drastically that little description of the actual events would be found. The traditional theory that John Mark, the companion of the apostle Peter, took down Peter's recollections and later wrote them up as a Gospel is to be preferred. That view has the support of all the early writers in the church as well as accounting for the facts of the Gospel quite satisfactorily.

Mark probably wrote his Gospel in Rome sometime before the civil war that took place there in A.D. 68-69. It was a difficult time for the church. Persecution had taken the lives of many prominent Christians, including the apostles Peter and Paul. No doubt Mark felt the time had arrived to put his material into a more permanent form. The style of writing has the appearance of being hastily done, without a lot of editing to smooth out the rough places. This gives the book a feeling of immediacy. Vivid detail, fast action, violent conflict, all are present in abundance. Mark used a literary device (the word *immediately*) to give this feeling of fast-paced activity. It occurs over 40 times.

Theological Themes

The purposes for Mark's writings are not hard to find. First, and in this case foremost, is to show us what the *gospel* is, namely, Jesus' life, death, and resurrection. The church was preaching a message of salvation in abbreviated form, and Mark wanted to show what the message was all about. It was the story of Jesus, the Incarnate Son of God, who died for our sins, was buried, and rose again. Mark spends no time at all on Jesus' birth, early years, or secondary life events. The story begins with the preaching of John the Baptist, moves quickly to Jesus' confrontation with authorities, and concentrates on the events of the last week of his life. Ten chapters are used for the first 30 years of Jesus' life, and six chapters are devoted to the last week. That gives an idea of what was important to Mark. It is not without reason that the church has chosen the cross as its symbol; the Gospel of Mark shows the reason why.

A second point that Mark wanted to make was that Jesus, Son of God though he was, was also human. Mark stressed the emotions of Jesus more than any other writer. Jesus is seen as one who was like us in every way, except for sin. Jesus got tired, hungry, weary, discouraged, was encouraged, strengthened, determined, and steadfast. All of us can identify with what Jesus went through because as human beings we have experienced similar feelings.

Third, Mark wrote to encourage Christians who were being persecuted. To see Jesus stand up in the face of opposition should give them the strength to do that too.

Finally, Mark wanted to show the power of Jesus. All through the Gospel we are able to see Jesus as he overcame demonic powers, disease, ignorance, enemies, and finally death. The Father stood by him, and he accomplished the task God had for him to do.

Outline
1. Prologue   *1:1-13*
2. Jesus' early ministry   *1:14–9:1*
3. Transfiguration and trip to Jerusalem
   9:2–10:52
4. Jesus' last week   *11:1–15:47*
5. Resurrection of Jesus   *16:1-8 (20)*

Luke
Author: Luke
Date: c. A.D. 65

Content

The third Gospel was written by an ancient
medical doctor named Luke, a traveling companion of the apostle Paul. He put together
what was evidently intended to be a history of
the Christian movement from its beginnings
up to his own day. It included the gospel about
Jesus of Nazareth as volume one; the Book of
Acts, which was about the work of the risen
Jesus in the lives of his followers as volume
two; and perhaps a volume three, which is
either lost to us today or was never written
because of the persecution that arose at that
time (in which Luke may have died). Peter and
Paul died at approximately that time so it is
possible that Luke did too.

The first four verses of Luke's gospel tell
us what was going on historically at the time
of writing, as well as how ancient writers went
about doing their job. Luke pointed out that
Christianity was of interest to a lot of people,
so much so that "many" had begun writing
histories of the movement (no doubt Mark was
one of them). That was good in a way, but also
worrisome. Luke was concerned that the truth
might get lost in all that was being written if
it were not carefully verified. Consequently,

he decided to make a careful study of what had
been said, checking the facts out with people
who had been around since the early days of
Jesus. The result of his research was this
Gospel that bears his name. He directed the
book to a Roman official named Theophilus,
no doubt to convince him that Christianity was
no threat to the empire, as well as being God's
appointed way of salvation.

Theological Themes

Luke's gospel has several characteristics.
First, Luke made a special point of relating
Jesus to world history. In his genealogy he
traced Christ's ancestors all the way back to
Adam, rather than just to David or Abraham,
as Matthew did. That would have meant very
little to a Gentile reader, but tracing Jesus to
Adam makes him part of all history, including
Gentile history.

Second, Luke was especially interested in
Jesus' birth and infancy. Matthew saw it as a
fulfillment of prophecy, Luke saw it as an
extraordinary event that took place in the
midst of secular history. He itemized six historical notes (3:1-2) intended to insure historical accuracy. The information is so precise in
this section of the Gospel that Mary, the
mother of Jesus, was probably the source of
much of it.

Third, Luke was concerned to stress the
relation of the kingdom of God to those in

need. He showed that Jesus brought good news for the poor, oppressed, sick, downtrodden, and captive. Jesus came to set men and women free from bondage and oppression. It is a spiritual message that touches all parts of our lives, including the social dimension.

Fourth, Luke was interested in women and in social relationships. He described the place that women played among Jesus' followers with sympathy and interest. He also realized that Jesus' acceptance of women went against some of the rules of his day. Jesus was not afraid to set new standards, especially for those who were not being treated properly.

Finally, Luke was concerned to show the universal dimension of the gospel of Christ. Matthew was, too, but he spoke as a Jew. Luke spoke as a Gentile, showing that the gospel is for everyone—men, women, slaves, free, Jews, Gentiles—whoever is in need is invited to come to Jesus to be saved.

Outline

1. Prologue *1:1-4*
2. Jesus' birth and early years *1:5–4:13*
3. Jesus' Galilean ministry *4:14–9:50*
4. Jesus' trip to Jerusalem *9:51–19:27*
5. Triumphal entry and last week in Jerusalem *19:28–23:56*
6. Resurrection and post-resurrection appearances of Jesus *24:1-53*

John

Author: John
Date: c. A.D. 95

Content

The Gospel of John does not have a name attached to it, but from earliest times it has been attributed to John the beloved apostle, one of the followers of Jesus. John had been a rather violent youth, getting a nickname somewhat akin to *Loudmouth*—"Son of Thunder," to be exact. His personal knowledge of Jesus, and the many years that had passed between Jesus' death and resurrection and the writing of his gospel, had transformed him into an apostle of love. No one speaks with more understanding about that aspect of God's nature than does John. He asserted that "God is love" (1 John 4:8) and that God loved the world so much that he gave his only Son for it (3:16). It is all the more striking that John should stress this in the light of the turbulent years through which he lived. Ultimately, John was sent to live on a deserted island, there to die.

John began his Gospel with an unusual prologue that is in effect a cosmic genealogy. It takes us back before the dawn of time, when only God existed, and there we are told that Christ, identified as "the Word," also existed. He was with God and was God (1:1). That proposition creates the foundation for what Christians have asserted from the earliest days of their existence, that Jesus was no less than God himself. Jesus, before coming to earth, was the possessor (and creator) of life, the one who conquered darkness (all forces of evil). He is the light that enlightens human minds (1:9) and opens the door to become children of God to those who take God at his word (1:12).

John continued his Gospel by recounting many of the facts also found in the other three Gospels, but with an extensive interpretation woven into it that draws out their inner meaning. He also recorded some incidents that were not mentioned by the others. There must have been a large number of stories circulating at that time, and John notes that if everything Jesus did was written down it would be hard to find room enough in the world for all the books about him (21:25).

One special section, chapters 14-17, in John's gospel has no parallel in the other Gospels. Only John has the section known as the "upper room discourse." In it Jesus speaks in the most personal terms imaginable about life, spirituality, prayer, hope, comfort, God, heaven, and joy. It is one of the favorite sections of the Bible, containing such familiar words as "I am the way and the truth and the life (14:7), and "Greater love has no one than this, that one lay down his life for his friends" (15:13).

Theological Themes

By writing his Gospel, John was trying to accomplish several things in addition to giving us some basic facts of Jesus' life. First, he was trying to show that Jesus was God. Many in his day (and in our own, too, for that matter) doubted this. It does seem to be an almost impossible thing to believe, but nothing less will do. Jesus was, and is, the eternal God of the universe, along with the Father and the Holy Spirit.

Second, John was stressing the human nature of Jesus. He was a man as well as God. He was born, lived in Palestine, drank water and ate food, grew weary with travel, suffered, and died. It was necessary for John to emphasize the humanity of Jesus because some thinkers in his day were looking on Jesus as merely passing through this world ghost-like, never really becoming part of it. John was stressing that only a real human being could save humankind.

Third, the Gospel was written specifically so that we might believe in Jesus and "have life in his name" (20:31). John was concerned that those who heard of Jesus should benefit by that knowledge.

Finally, John wanted to emphasize the close relationship between Jesus and his followers. He is the good shepherd and we are his sheep; he is the door through which we enter life; he is the bread of life that feeds our souls; he is the water of life that cures our

deepest thirst; he is the vine of which we are
the branches. All those figures of speech were
intended to help us see that without Jesus we
can do nothing. As we live in that realization,
our joy will be complete (15:11).

Outline

The Dispersion of Jewish Communities in Christ's Time

Chronology of New Testament Books

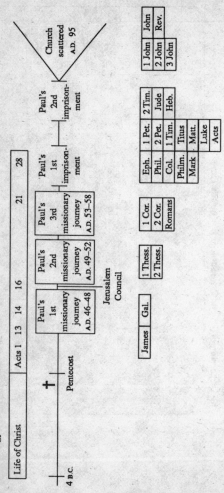

ACTS

Acts
Author: Luke
Date: c. A.D. 65

Content

Luke wrote the Book of Acts as a continuation of his history of the church. Volume one, which we know as the Gospel of Luke, tells about Jesus and the establishment of Christianity by his death and resurrection. Volume two, the Book of Acts, picks up with the ascension of Jesus back to heaven and the spread of the gospel out from Jerusalem, ultimately to Rome, where the book ends. It is not known whether or not Luke intended a volume three which would have gone to the end of the apostles' lives. It is possible that he never lived to complete the work, even if that was his intention.

The reasons Luke wrote the Book of Acts are not hard to find. First, he wanted to present the facts about the new movement. Much was being said about it that was false, and Luke wanted to correct any misimpressions that might have existed.

Second, he may have wanted to show Theophilus, to whom the book was dedicated, that as a Roman official he need not fear what Christianity might do. Granted when it went to some places trouble arose, but it was not the fault of the believers. They were trying to live peaceably, and within the law. It was usually the pagans who rose up in protest causing the difficulties.

Third, Luke wanted to show how the two primary leaders of the church, Peter and Paul, exercised their ministry. Because of some misunderstandings about the relations between the two, some people were trying to create separate churches. Luke tried to show that they were not in opposition to each other, but in fact agreed on the basic point at issue, namely, whether a person needed to become a Jew in order to become a Christian. Both said

Paul's First Missionary Journey

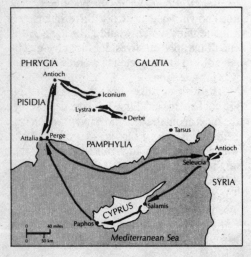

that it was not necessary, and so did the rest of the church (15:1-21).

Finally, Luke wanted to chart the progress of the gospel from Jerusalem to Syria, to Asia Minor, to Macedonia and Greece (Europe), and finally to Rome. It was Paul's desire to see the gospel go to all people, and this was a fulfillment of his dreams. It is ironic that he went as a prisoner rather than freely, but he saw God's hand in it. He wanted to make it to Rome, one way or another, and this was how God decided to do it. So Paul, the prisoner, preached freedom in Christ.

The book divides easily into two sections, the first half dealing with events in and around Jerusalem (1:1–12:25) and the second half with the spread of the gospel out from there (13:1–28:31).

Paul's Second Missionary Journey

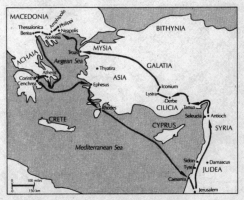

Theological Themes

The first half of Acts stresses some important theological points. The message is rooted in the Old Testament, as would be expected, because the preaching was primarily to Jews. There was also a strong emphasis on the death and resurrection of Jesus. This point could be made forcefully because it was in the very place where those events took place and many people there remembered it well. There was also a special focus on coming judgment and the end of the age. The judgment was to come sooner than most expected it, with the fall of Jerusalem in A.D. 70. Finally, there was an urgent call to repentance and faith.

In the second half of the book, new theological insights are added to what is found in the first part. Because the gospel had gone

Paul's Third Missionary Journey

beyond the bounds of Palestine, follow-up was stressed. That was necessary if the church was to grow. It isn't enough to preach the gospel and leave; one must make sure that the church's continuing needs are met. Also, the organizational structure of the church must be attended to. The church is not a place where anyone can be anything or one person rules like a despot. It is a place where the Spirit of God directs life and worship in an orderly manner through proper organizational structures.

Finally, new ways of expressing the message were needed. Because most of the converts outside Palestine were Gentiles, they would not be familiar with the Old Testament or its ideas. Ways to communicate to them, without changing the essential nature of the gospel, had to be found. What was done by the early missionaries in the Book of Acts sets a pattern for all of us to follow.

Outline

1. Early days of the church *1:1–2:47*
2. The gospel in Jerusalem *3:1–7:60*
3. Spread of the gospel to Samaria, Joppa, Caesarea, and Antioch *8:1–12:25*
4. Missionary journeys of Paul *13:1–21:16*
5. Arrest of Paul and journey to Rome *21:17–28:31*

Paul's Journey to Rome

THE EPISTLES (LETTERS)

Romans
Author: Paul
Date: c. A.D. 58

Content
The Book of Romans is one of the most important, carefully-put-together, and theological books in the New Testament. The apostle Paul was evidently thinking about the great city of the ancient world, Rome, and although he had never been there he wanted to explain the nature of the Christian movement to them. He wrote in sweeping terms, covering the span of history and thought from Adam to the end of the age.

Theological Themes
Paul believed that God created the world and the first human beings as a kind of representative for all humanity. From Adam came the human race—but, alas, not as perfect, but imperfect, subject to sin and death. Sin and death are also our own choices, showing that we are truly our father's children. This fact has made the world a difficult place in which to live. Some people have sunk to extraordinary depths, giving up worship of God for worship of animals, snakes, or idols. No doubt Paul was reflecting on what he saw in many cities

through which he had traveled, where such things were common. Not only had some individuals debased worship, they also debased human relationships, giving in to violent and unnameable passions toward one another. Essentially Paul saw this as unthankfulness to God, who made us for glory and virtue. We *prefer* our degraded abuse of one another and of creation rather than the glory of God. Not every one has fallen that low, but all are sinful nonetheless. Paul summed this up by saying, "all have sinned and fall short of the glory of God" (3:23).

In spite of our desperate situation, God has not abandoned us. Two things stand out. First, God can still be known by sinful human beings; God still speaks to us. There is evidence of God to be seen in creation, as well as a law written within our hearts that speaks to us of higher things. Second, God has done the seemingly impossible for us; he has made salvation available in Christ. Jesus died for us, who did not deserve it, so that we might be brought back to God—and all without compromise on God's part.

To benefit by this salvation offered to us, all we need to do is accept it. Paul thus says that the gospel is the power of God unto salvation to everyone who believes (1:16). To the one who does not "work" (for salvation) but who believes what God has done in Christ, his or her faith is accepted as righteousness (4:5). If we confess that Jesus is our Lord, believing that God raised him from the dead, we will be saved (10:9-10). Paul believed this strongly because earlier, when he was practicing his Jewish religion, he had tried to earn his salvation but had failed. Martin Luther later found out the same thing when he tried to earn salvation by following monastic rules. Rules, whether Jewish, pagan, or Christian, don't save; only God saves.

Paul followed those insights with a lengthy discussion on the benefits of the Christian life and how to live it. The benefits are beautifully described in chapter 8 in detail. Let two points suffice to summarize the whole. First, God never ceases to love us. Nothing in all the creation can separate us from the ruler of creation (8:37-39). Second, God is able to work good for us in all things (8:28). It is not possible to explain exactly how God can do this, but because he is God, he can, and we become aware that he does this as we trust him. There is also a discussion of how to work out our Christian life in practical ways (chapters 12-15).

An important part of the Book of Romans is Paul's discussion of Israel and the church (chapters 9-11). He was trying to show that God was at work all through history, but especially in Israel. That brought up the problem of why God seemed to set certain people aside. Paul showed that this is only an apparent dilemma. In actual fact, only the *believers* in Israel were really Israel, and the believers in

Jesus now continue as the spiritual Israel. But that did not mean that Israel as a nation was set aside utterly. In some mysterious way, when God's dealings with the Gentiles are over, all Israel will be saved (11:25-26).

The Book of Romans is a theological and practical guide for the believer. To learn its secrets is to learn the essence of being a Christian.

Outline
1. Greeting *1:1-7*
2. All the world is sinful *1:8–3:20*
3. The fact of salvation *3:21–5:21*
4. Salvation applied *6:1–8:39*
5. Israel and the church *9:1–11:36*
6. Guidelines for the believer *12:1–15:33*
7. Closing greetings *16:1-27*

1 Corinthians
Author: Paul
Date: c. A.D. 56

Content
Paul traveled to Corinth on his second missionary journey and spent some time there establishing the church. It was a difficult task, not only because of the opposition that he met, but because of the city itself. Corinth was notorious even in ancient times for being a city of great evil. As a seaport, it attracted all kinds of people who would work their evil, depart without being held accountable, and leave behind misery and distress. When people in that setting became Christians, they were transformed into new creations in Christ. But regrettably, some brought along many of their old habits.

Theological Themes
It is important to remember that when we believe, we are not usually transformed instantly into something totally other than what we were before. We are new creations, but we need to "grow in grace" with the power that God gives us. It is the power of God that makes the difference, and it is there if we will avail ourselves of it. Some of the Corinthian Christians did, but many did not.

A large portion of this book is devoted to Paul's responding to questions put to him by representatives from Corinth. They cover a spectrum of theological and practical problems. First, Paul dealt with the relationship of faith to life, showing that faith is the essence of Christian existence. It might seem foolish to some, but it is in fact the only way to live a life that is pleasing to God. Paul continued by discussing how we are then to work this out and what rewards we will receive. In a metaphorical description of judgment (3:10-15), Paul showed that some of our acts will not survive the test. But some will, and, like precious stones, will shine forever. A very important passage about living nonjudgmentally opens chapter 4. We are not to pass judgment on each other; only God can do that. Paul then took up a series of problems—lawsuits, personal grievances, immorality, issues related to marriage, eating food that had been sacrificed to idols, human freedom to act as we please; then he went on to discuss the Lord's supper, spiritual gifts, and the doctrine of the resurrection.

Paul's discussion of spiritual gifts is especially important. Three chapters outline how our gifts are to be exercised (chapters 12-14). Here is a partial list of the gifts that the Spirit distributes among believers and the constructive use of them. Paul stressed the motive that should underlie the use of anything God gives us: love (chapter 13). If we possessed all the brilliance or strength in the world and did not live lovingly, we would be nothing at all.

The discussion on the resurrection (chapter 15) is equally important. It is not just today that people are inclined to doubt the truth of what Christians say about Jesus' coming back from the dead. It was also true in Paul's day. He found it necessary to defend the doctrine of Christ's bodily resurrection. It is the foundation of the Christian faith that Jesus died and rose again. Based on that, we have eternal hope.

Paul concluded his letter with a series of greetings and an exhortation to make a contribution to the church in Jerusalem. That might sound like a small matter, but in fact it was very important to Paul. He wanted the early Christians to recognize their dependence on one another. The gospel had come from Jerusalem and had been a spiritual benefit to the Corinthians. They, in turn, were to accept some responsibility for those who were suffering there. In that way both groups would recognize the oneness they had in Christ. If more of this spirit were evident today, we would have far fewer problems.

Outline

2 Corinthians

Author: Paul
Date: c. A.D. 57

Content

This letter was written by the apostle Paul shortly after he wrote 1 Corinthians. He had received word from Corinth about how the first letter had been received and was responding to that. It is probably the most personal and emotional of his letters.

The first thing he wanted to do was to reestablish his place as apostle to the Corinthians. Some persons were attacking his authority; others were fragmenting the church. Paul wanted them to realize that he had nothing personal to gain by preaching to them; what he was doing was for their good. Not only that, he did it at great cost to himself. He listed some of the things he had gone through (6:3-10; 11:23-29), including beatings and imprisonments. His desire to have authority was not for his sake, but theirs. They needed someone to lead them through the darkness into the light. As for those who were splitting the church, a simple look at the results would show they were on the wrong track. Strife and discord are never the result of the work of God's Spirit, only of selfish people.

Theological Themes

Paul made a special point of emphasizing Christ's death for us and the glory of salvation. Our helpless condition resulted in God's sending his Son to save us. It was God's love that moved him to help us and that moved Paul to preach the gospel (5:14). The work that Christ did on the cross was world-changing. He did not die simply to be an example of dedication to a cause, but to reconcile the world to God. We had gone astray in error and sin. It required that a drastic step be taken to bring us back, and that was taken by Jesus as he died for our sins (5:19). Now, if we believe in him, we may become part of the new creation, renewed in Christ (5:17). The offer has been made; the right moment to accept it is the moment it is understood; later might be too late (6:1-2).

A good part of this letter is devoted to living the Christian life. This material is not found in one place, as is the case in some of Paul's other letters, but is scattered throughout. Paul again made mention of sexual irregularities and the necessity to keep ourselves only for God's use; that means solely for our marriage partners. Our bodies are temples of the Holy Spirit and ought not to be abused (6:14–7:1). We are also to support those who minister to us. Paul had earlier used an ox grinding out the grain as an example. The Old Testament forbade the muzzling of an ox while it was working, because it needed nourishment to continue. If God cares for oxen, does he not also care for human beings who give unselfishly of themselves for the benefit of others?

Finally, Paul spoke of some of his own struggles. He hinted at his physical problems only in one other place (Gal. 4:12-15), but here he went into some detail, explaining how he had begged God for healing but did not receive it (12:1-10). He did receive something even more important, however—a meeting with God that made him a stronger person. He learned how to achieve *through* suffering, rather than flee the suffering and live apart from it. There is a great mystery in this, but it is often only when we willingly accept our burden, whatever it is, that we grow to maturity and overcome it in the end. Paul learned that our weakness is the opportunity for God's strength to manifest itself.

Outline

Galatians
Author: Paul
Date: c. A.D. 48

Content

The letter to the Galatians is probably the first
letter the apostle Paul wrote. He had made a
missionary trip to the churches in that region
(Galatia), which was described by Luke in
Acts 13–14. The major cities Paul preached at
were Antioch, Lystra, Iconium, and Derbe,
important centers of population and trade.
Paul felt it important to preach the gospel to
such strategic crossroads. That way travelers
could be reached who would carry the gospel
back to their own countries. Paul was not
received well by those cities, however. The
Jews listened at first because Paul was also a
Jew, but their willingness to listen changed
when Paul began speaking about Jesus as the
Messiah. The Gentiles became hostile when
Paul rejected their paganism. At Lystra Paul
was savagely attacked and left for dead. In
spite of that, a number of people believed and
the church was established in the region of
Galatia.

A serious problem arose, prompting the
writing of this letter. Some strong-minded
Jewish Christians had arrived in Galatia to
undermine Paul's authority. They were of the
opinion that a person could not be saved if he
were not circumcised according to Jewish cus-

tom. They said that Paul was arrogant, a liar, had not told the Galatians the whole truth, was weak and sickly, and a coward. The Galatians were beginning to waver in their allegiance to Paul and in their acceptance of his gospel preaching. Because of those circumstances, Paul wrote the letter now titled "Galatians."

Theological Themes

The central message of the letter to the Galatians is that a person is saved by faith alone; being saved means being free. Being saved by faith alone is the heart of the gospel. Paul made his case by showing that Abraham was saved by faith (a good example because the Jews considered Abraham the father of their nation). This is the way God has established the salvation of humankind. Jesus died so that we would not have to earn our own salvation—which we could not do even if we wanted to. To deny that we can be saved by faith is to deny God himself.

When a person believes, that person becomes free—free from the penalty of sin, from useless rules, from the law, from evil powers, from himself or herself. It is a message that opens the door to meaningful life and joy. The Holy Spirit enters, bringing "love, joy, peace, patience, kindness, goodness, faithfulness, gentleness, and self-control" (5:22-23). A person can then live for others, loving them and bearing their burdens. Freedom to be what

God wants and to serve others is the heart of the Christian life.

Paul defended his point that we are saved by faith and made free by an elaborate set of arguments. He showed that his apostleship entitled him to speak with authority, that the risen Jesus had revealed the truth to him, that the other apostles in Jerusalem agreed, that the Old Testament taught what he was teaching, that the Holy Spirit affirmed the truth of his message by working miracles, and that this gospel worked in life. Anyone who did not agree should be careful so as not to be fighting against God. Whatever persons sow, that will they reap. A life of faith brings life. A life of self-seeking and evil brings death. The choice is always before us, and Paul urges that we choose life.

Outline

1. Introduction *1:1-9*
2. Paul's defense of his apostleship *1:10–2:10*
3. Paul's defense of his gospel *2:11-21*
4. Salvation and its benefits *3:1–4:31*
5. The freedom that Christ brings *5:1–6:18*

Ephesians
Author: Paul
Date: c. A.D. 60 or 61

Content
The city of Ephesus, one of the great cities of
antiquity, was located on the western coast of
Asia Minor, in present-day Turkey. It is no
longer of any consequence. All that remains
are some magnificent ruins, now being ex-
cavated by numerous organizations from
around the world. Because the main roads,
buildings, temples, houses, and amphitheater
are more or less intact, one may get the feel of
what it must have been like to live in Roman
times by wandering among those extraordinary remains of a past civilization.

Paul traveled to Ephesus on his second
journey and left Priscilla and Aquila there to
engage in ministry (Acts 18:18-19). They
must have done a good job because when Paul
arrived later to stay for almost three years, he
found a growing Christian community (Acts
19:1-10). Paul was forced to leave the city
after a violent uprising of the people because
of loss of money for the local temple of Artemis (Diana), which was blamed on his
having said that idols were nothing and ought
not to be supported. The temple, one of the
great monuments of antiquity, must have
brought an enormous amount of money into
Ephesus by the worshipers of Artemis. A

touching sermon is recorded in Acts 20:17-38, in which Paul encouraged the Ephesian elders to remain in the ways of the Lord. It is also a beautiful portrait of Paul the missionary and his love for the church.

The letter to the Ephesians was written by Paul near the end of his life while he was in prison in Rome. It is important to keep the serenity and peace of the letter in mind. Paul's sense of calm came from the presence of the Lord, not from his external circumstances. The letter was probably intended as a circular letter to be passed on from church to church for everyone's instruction.

Theological Themes

The Book of Ephesians makes numerous important theological points, mainly dealing with the nature of salvation and the Christian life. The first chapter stresses the comprehensive nature of salvation. In one of the longest sentences of the Bible (1:3-14; see KJV—other versions divide it up), Paul spoke of the eternal purpose of God. God planned, executed, sustains, and directs our salvation. The only reason given for God's electing some to be saved is his love. From the depth of God's being there poured forth compassion and grace that resulted in the salvation of those who believe. Chapter 2 continues this theme, broadening it to explain how Jew and Gentile are now made one in Christ. No barriers should keep human beings apart; all are alike in God's eyes. Love does not discriminate but freely blesses the object of its affection. Chapter 3 continues with an emphasis on Paul's gospel and how it related to the overall mystery of God. The riches of Christ, which are past finding out, are made available to us if we will reach out and take them. When one does this he or she enters into the love of Christ, with knowledge that goes beyond words and experience. To know it is enough. Chapters 4 through 6 contain teachings about Christian living. Paul touches on marriage, family, temptation, anger, service, and spiritual conflict. In all of this the solution is to know Christ better in practical experience. Prayer becomes a key to winning the victory over sin, evil, Satan, and our own wayward selves.

Outline
1. The glorious nature of salvation *1:1-23*
2. The unity of all who believe in Christ *2:1-22*
3. The mystery of the love of Christ *3:1-21*
4. The nature of the Christian life *4:1–6:24*

Philippians
Author: Paul
Date: c. A.D. 60 or 61

Content
Paul wrote the letter to the Philippians while
in prison in Rome. He had visited the city on
his second missionary journey as described in
Acts 16:11-40. Paul had been fairly well
received there until he cast the demon out of
a slave girl who made money for her owner by
foretelling the future. Paul and his companion
Silas were then beaten and thrown into prison.
An earthquake opened the doors, but they did
not escape. As a result the jailer was converted
when he heard the gospel. Paul made use of
his Roman citizenship to gain his freedom on
the following day.

Theological Themes
The letter Paul wrote to his friends at Philippi
is one of the most personal in the New Testament. It does not begin with the usual assertion
of authority (Paul, an apostle . . .), but rather,
"Paul and Timothy, servants of Christ Jesus."
The theme of the book is that of rejoicing in
the Lord. No fewer than eight times does Paul
speak about how we are to rejoice in spite of
our circumstances (1:18; 2:17; 2:18; 2:28; 3:1;
4:4). It must be remembered that Paul was in
prison at the time with little hope of release,

virtually alone, weary from his labors of preaching the gospel, and without funds. How remarkable that Paul should stress the gratitude and joy we ought to have. He was able to do that because he had learned the secret of rejoicing, namely, we are to rejoice *in the Lord.* Because God does not change and is our loving heavenly Father, we need not fear. God has everything under control, so whether we are in abundance or in want, we may be content (4:1-12).

Paul also stressed his certainty that God who began the work in each believer would bring it to completion. If it were left up to us, it would be in great doubt. But because God will never fail us or push us beyond what we are able to bear, we will be able to see life through (1:6). This does not mean that we are to sit down and do nothing. We are to work out our own salvation with fear and trembling (2:12), pressing toward the goal of the upward call of God in Christ (3:14).

Another point that Paul made is that heaven awaits the believer upon death. Paul was not being morbid about it, but he realized that we all must face death sooner or later. For the believer death should hold no terrors (1:21). To die is gain because we will be entering into the presence of Jesus who loves us and gave himself for us. Paul did not know it at the time, but within a few years he was to die in the city of Rome. Paul used the life of Jesus as a model for believers to follow (2:5-11). Though Jesus was in glory with the Father he left it to die on the cross for all who would believe in him. Because of that, someday every knee will bow and every tongue confess that Jesus Christ is Lord.

The value of prayer was stressed by Paul as the way to have true freedom from anxiety (4:4-7). The peace of God will be given to those who offer themselves to God in simple commitment. Paul gave up everything else, he said, in order to know Christ, the power of his resurrection, and the fellowship of his suffering and death (3:10).

Outline
1. Salutation and opening prayer *1:1-11*
2. Paul's knowledge of Christ *1:12-30*
3. The example of Christ *2:1-11*
4. Exhortations and defense of himself *2:12-3:21*
5. The secret of rejoicing *4:1-23*

Colossians

Author: Paul
Date: c. A.D. 60 or 61

Content

Paul wrote this letter while he was in prison in
Rome. It is part of a group of letters called "the
prison letter" (Philippians, Ephesians, and
Philemon). There is no evidence that Paul had
ever been to Colosse, but he obviously knew
people there. Probably they were converted in
Ephesus, a nearby city, when Paul was minis-
tering there on his third missionary journey.
He had been there for about two and a half
years, and Luke records that all the residents
of Asia (Asia Minor, which includes Colosse)
heard the word of the Lord (Acts 19:10). The
letter itself is not as personal as some of Paul's
other letters, and understandably so. He does
mention a special messenger, Epaphras, who
is the link between him and the church there
(1:7), as well as a series of other people whom
he knew (4:10-17).

As is true with many of Paul's letters,
Colossians may be divided into two major
sections, the first doctrinal and the second
practical. It is significant that Paul's letters are
often arranged this way, with doctrine coming
first. Correct teaching must always be the
foundation for correct action. Doctrine or
teaching alone would lead to narrowness and
self-righteousness. Practice or action alone

would lead to conflict and error. Together, with correct doctrine as the foundation, it is possible to lead a life that is pleasing to God, ourselves, and others.

Theological Themes

The main emphasis in the doctrinal section of this letter is on what theologians call Christology, or the doctrine of Christ. Paul wanted to emphasize the unique nature of Jesus. Jesus was the image, or express reflection, of the invisible God. He was involved in the creation of the world and of all things in it. He is also party to sustaining it in existence. Nothing exists apart from Christ. He is also the head or ruler of the church. Paul was stressing that the eternal, divine qualities of God, which might have been hidden forever from us, have been made known in Jesus, who became one of us. But two things need to be said about his coming to earth.

First, it was not in the way that most pious Jews expected. He came to conquer evil in all its forms, but he came as a servant of God who was willing to die. It was, in fact, the death of Jesus that was the undoing of evil (2:13-15). To those who are capable of believing it, the truth is there. If we would forget ourselves and live for God and others, we would find true life. Jesus pointed the way by dying for our sins and rising again.

Second, Jesus' self-sacrifice was not simply for us to look at and think about. It was designed by God to make us better people. As believers in Christ, we have everything we need to live our lives. He freed us from all evil forces, he is seated at God's right hand for us, and we are to set our minds on things above, not on things below (3:1-4).

The practical material follows this doctrinal material and in some cases is mixed in with it. It deals with how we are to live our Christian lives; how to have personal peace; comments about parents, wives, husbands, and children; matters of prayer, personal purity, and Christian freedom.

Outline
1. Opening salutation and prayer *1:1-12*
2. Christological teaching *1:13–2:15*
3. Practical implications of Christology *2:16–4:6*
4. Closing remarks and greetings *4:7-18*

Distances of Key New Testament Cities from Jerusalem

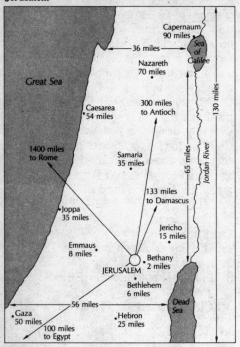

1 Thessalonians
Author: Paul
Date: c. A.D. 50-51

Content

Paul wrote this letter to the Thessalonians
from Corinth a short time after preaching there
on his second missionary journey. There had
been a great deal of persecution of the
believers that began while Paul was still there.
Apparently a group of violent men had
decided that it was their responsibility to destroy this new movement. They were, in ac-
tuality, afraid of it and how it might change
their evil lives. It is often the case that opposition is based on fear and misunderstanding,
rather than on reason. Had these men thought
about it, it would have been to their advantage
as well as to the advantage of their city to have
Christianity there. At any rate, Paul had
traveled on, having been run off from Thes-
salonica, and ended up in Corinth. Then he
sent Timothy back to find out how things were
going. The good news that all was well was a
great relief to him, prompting him to write. He
thanked them for their concern for him and
went on to straighten out some misunderstandings over doctrine that had arisen.

Theological Themes

Paul began his letter by commending the church for their spiritual activity and witness. What they were doing was being talked about in other places and was a good example for others to follow. In this they were following Paul's good example, who in turn, was following the Lord. Paul was aware of how difficult it is to remain faithful, especially in the midst of heavy persecution, and was deeply thankful to God for the way they were continuing in their commitment. He reminded them that Jesus not only delivered us from our sins, but will deliver us from all evil when he returns again.

Paul continued this theme by speaking about his own ministry and how it was for him. He, too, had been persecuted so he understood what they were going through. Others, too, had suffered for Christ, notably, the believers in Judea (the land of Israel). It had never been easy to be a Christian, and Paul wanted to share his confidence with these new followers of the Lord. He spoke in a very personal way, telling them that his care for them was like that of a nurse for her children or a father for his sons. In all of this there was the practical intent of helping the Thessalonians live a better life.

A special problem regarding marriage and personal holiness had arisen, so Paul dealt specially with that. The ancient world was notoriously lax in such matters, creating severe problems for those who were trying to keep everything in the proper places in their lives. With the grace and strength of God, Paul said, they would be able to overcome those temptations and obstacles to Christian growth.

Paul spent the last part of his letter discussing a serious misunderstanding that had arisen about the second coming of Jesus. It is difficult to know exactly what the problem was, but it evidently took two forms. First, some people were confused about who would benefit by Christ's return, assuming that only the *living* would be included. Those who died before Jesus came back would simply be left out. Second, others were worried about *when* Christ would come back, to the point of no longer working; they became a burden on the rest of the church. Paul set those two problems straight and went on to stress the *fact* of Christ's return and what that should mean to us. It is a certainty that will terminate this age, bringing comfort to believers and judgment to unbelievers. We are to live expectantly, joyfully, and courageously in the light of its near occurrence.

Outline

1. Paul's greetings and exhortations to the Thessalonians *1:1–2:20*
2. Paul's rejoicing over Timothy's report *3:1-13*
3. Moral questions handled *4:1-12*
4. The coming of Christ and the day of the Lord *4:13–5:28*

2 Thessalonians
Author: Paul
Date: c. A.D. 51

Content
After Paul had written his first letter to the
Thessalonians he received word that further
confusion had arisen in the church there about
the doctrine of the second coming of Christ.
Seemingly it was reported that Paul himself
had sent the information, or at least was the
source of it. In addition to that, some people
were thinking that the coming of Christ was
so near that it was no longer necessary to
support oneself or one's family. Why work if
Christ is about to end the world? To deal with
those issues, as well as to encourage believers,
Paul wrote a second letter, probably within a
few months of having written his first letter.

Theological Themes
Paul began by encouraging the Thessalonians
in the midst of their persecutions. He pointed
out that they were called to be worthy of the
kingdom of God for which they were currently
suffering. If they bore up under it, when Christ
returned they would be comforted and their
persecutors would feel the judging hand of
God. On the day when Christ returns he will
be glorified among his saints and will banish

from his presence all who have rejected the gospel (1:5-12).

Paul went on to say that the coming of Christ would not take place without some other events happening first. It is a mistake, Paul said, to imagine that the Second Coming can happen without relation to the rest of the plan of God. Christ's return must be preceded by a general falling away (or apostasy); the unveiling of a "man of lawlessness," usually called the Antichrist, and his attempts at universal domination. The Antichrist is already at work in spirit, but he must be manifested as such before the end can come. After these things take place, the Lord Jesus will return to destroy him (2:8).

Paul followed this explanation with ethical exhortations of a practical sort. The doctrine of Christ's coming is not to make us lazy, arrogant, or immoral, but busy, humble, and pure. We are not to be weary in well-doing (3:6-13).

Outline
1. The glorious coming of Christ reaffirmed
   1:1-12
2. The events that must precede Christ's
   coming *2:1-17*
3. Exhortations to holy living in the light of
   Christ's return *3:1-18*

1 Timothy

Author: Paul
Date: c. A.D. 64

Content

After Paul's release from prison in A.D. 62, he spent about two years traveling (some early sources say as far as Spain), both preaching the gospel and encouraging the churches that were in existence. He was rearrested in 64 and probably died in that year. Sometime between his two imprisonments Paul wrote three letters (1, 2 Timothy, and Titus) called the "pastoral letters" to his associates in Ephesus and on the island of Crete. Timothy seems to have been the younger of the two men and with a single church; Titus appears to have been an ambassador of some sort whose job it was to appoint elders and oversee the affairs of many churches.

Paul's first letter is basically practical, dealing with matters related to living a Christian life. There is also important doctrinal material. False views were developing. Some individuals wanted to establish little empires for themselves independently of the established churches.

Theological Themes

In a short summary of who Jesus was, Paul outlined some essentials of the faith (3:16).

Christian faith is a profound mystery; God alone knows all there is to know. Our job is to trust God and not worry about things over which we have no control. Christ's incarnation and resurrection are at the heart of what we believe. Jesus could have remained forever one with the Father in all his eternal glory, but that would have meant our eternal loss. But because of his love for us, he was willing to leave all that temporarily behind so that he might bring us to salvation. Paul's short doctrinal abstract ends with an emphasis on Christ's ascension and the preaching of the gospel to the world.

Paul also reiterated other theological points such as the place of prayer, the resurrection, the nature of God, and the benefits of the death of Christ.

The practical material in this letter covers two areas, public church life and private existence. The material about church life should be studied carefully by anyone who aspires to be a church officer. Paul listed the requirements for those who want to serve as bishops (or elders) and deacons. There are some differences in the requirements but basically they require that a person be wholly committed in life and heart. There is also a leader designated to look after the widows, an unusually large category of women in antiquity. The fact that there are church officers indicates that we all have a need for order and regularity. Just as a household or a business cannot run well without leaders and regulations, so the church must have its officers, guided by the Spirit and answerable to God and the people.

The material devoted to practical Christian living covers human relationships and actions. There is material for children, parents, husbands, wives, and servants. There is also a stress on freedom properly exercised. Evidently there were some who wanted to run the lives of others, but Paul would not allow that. We are to make up our own minds about what to eat or drink, whether to marry and how to handle our affairs (4:1-10). Our basic human needs are not to be despised because God made us this way. But they are not to dominate us, turning us into gluttons, drunkards, or adulterers. Everything must be put in its proper place under the guidance of the Spirit and with an attitude of humility.

Outline

1. Greetings and charge to Timothy *1:1-20*
2. Church officers and worship *2:1–3:16*
3. General regulations *4:1-16*
4. Specific regulations and instructions *5:1–6:10*
5. Final charge to Timothy *6:11-21*

2 Timothy
Author: Paul
Date: c. A.D. 64-66

Content
Paul's second letter to Timothy was probably
the last one he wrote. He had been arrested and
was in prison (4:6), knowing that the end was
at hand. It is a letter filled with courage and
strength, showing us what kind of person Paul
really was—or, better, what kind of person
God can help us to be if we trust in him. The
letter consists basically of four charges
directed to Timothy from the aged Paul.

Theological Themes
In the first charge, Paul reminded Timothy of
his godly heritage. His grandmother and
mother had set a wonderful example and
Timothy was to follow it. It is impossible to
overestimate the influence of our homes and
parents. As parents and others live godly lives,
younger ones absorb that atmosphere and become like that themselves. When we are parents our task is to continue that pattern so our
children will live before the Lord as well. It is
significant that Paul singled out the two
women for commendation, whether because
the father was an unbeliever or deceased. In
any case, by the grace of God, one parent can
do it if necessary.

That charge continues with Paul reminding Timothy to rekindle his gift. We have all been given endowments by God, but they must be used. If they are not, they will wither and die, like an unused muscle. If we exercise our gifts, they will grow and be strengthened. In Timothy's case this included defending the faith against error.

The second charge is in essence a command to be strong in God's grace. Paul used a marvelous collection of metaphors to describe the Christian life. A Christian is like a soldier whose task it is to do his commander's will. No soldier would dare go off on his own in the midst of battle, nor would a faithful Christian desert his post when engaged in fighting evil. Paul had used this metaphor before, describing it as the armor of God that we are to wear as we stand against the evil of our day (Eph. 6:1-17). The Christian is also like an athlete who prepares for the race, runs hard, and goes by the rules. We too must remember that, as Christians, discipline and honesty count for a great deal if we are to succeed. Finally, the Christian is like a farmer who breaks up the stubborn earth to bring out the best that is in it. A farmer's life is never easy, but the rewards are worth it. So too, for a Christian, we put our hand to the plow and do not turn back. In all of those figures we have before us the example of Jesus Christ.

The third charge is to be watchful over the flock and vigilant concerning the world. God has all kinds of people in his church and all must be cared for. As for ourselves we are to shun evil passions, live with a pure heart, and avoid controversies. The servant of God must not be quarrelsome and bigoted. If one is, that is a sure sign that God is not there. With respect to the world, God's servant must be aware of its evil and refuse to be a part of it. In the world there will be greed, arrogance, hatred, and indecency. Those sins must be kept out of the life of the church and of Christians. The tragedy is that sometimes these very things are to be found even among believers. When that happens, they must be compassionately but firmly dealt with.

Paul's fourth charge is to preach the word and be an example to the congregation. We are to be ready at all times to do whatever needs to be done to accomplish God's will. Paul closed this section with the memorable words, "I have fought the good fight, I have finished the race, I have kept the faith" (4:7). Timothy was to remember that he was not alone. Others had gone before him, setting an example for him.

Outline

Titus
Author: Paul
Date: c. A.D. 64-66

Content

Between Paul's two imprisonments in the early A.D. 60s, he traveled throughout the Mediterranean area. He went at least once to the important island of Crete but was appalled by what he found there. The church was weak, disorganized, corrupt, and under the influence of the society around it. After he left, Paul wanted to stay in touch. His letter is short, personal, and filled with practical advice.

Theological Themes

One of the fundamental problems facing the church concerned authority. It simply did not work when there was no reasonable organization. As a result, Titus needed to explain to the congregation how elders were to be chosen and how they were to function. But it was not just the church elders who needed instruction. All those whose lives had an impact on the church were in need of correction, from older adults to young people. To be Christians means that Christ has changed our lives. Those attitudes ought to be evident by our actions and attitudes.

Paul continued his exhortation by stressing that Christians are to be good citizens. We are not to give in to evil rulers, but we are to be willing to live according to the laws of whatever land we live in. Not to do this is to bring discredit on the gospel.

Paul concluded with a series of ethical exhortations in the light of Jesus' coming again. He came once to provide salvation for the world; he will come again to bless his people and judge the world. In the light of this, we are to be pure and zealous for good works (2:11-14). We have been saved by God's mercy, not according to our deeds, but in order to do good deeds. The order is important. We do not live Christian lives in order to be saved, but when we are saved, we live godly lives.

Outline

Philemon
Author: Paul
Date: c. A.D. 61

Content

Philemon was a friend of the apostle Paul who lived at Colosse, was a fellow worker in the gospel, and had a church in his house. He was a wealthy man who owned at least one slave, Onesimus. Onesimus had escaped from Philemon and after making his way to Rome was converted by the ministry of Paul. There is no need to speculate on how he met Paul. Probably, friendless and alone in a foreign city, he sought out the only person whose name he knew, Paul. At any rate, Onesimus was now going back, bearing this brief letter from Paul to Philemon, asking forgiveness and reinstatement. Paul expressed his desire that Onesimus now be truly *useful*—a play on words, because the name Onesimus means "useful," something he had hardly been in the past (v. 11).

The letter is important for at least two reasons. First, it shows how the preaching of the gospel changes lives. Paul, Philemon, Onesimus, Apphia, Archippus, Timothy, Epaphras, Mark, and Aristarchus, all mentioned by name, had been brought to new life in Christ. Where would these people have been without the Lord? Where would any of us be without the Lord? It is easy to forget that many great saints of the church were once pagan blasphemers who reviled the name of Christ. But in the mercy of God they came to a true knowledge of the risen Christ, who saved them and gave them new life.

Second, the basis for vast social change is implicit in the gospel of Christ. When Paul says "[take] him back for good—no longer a slave, but better than a slave, as a dear brother" (vv. 15-16), the deep human prejudices are forced to give way. In Christ there is "neither Jew nor Greek, slave nor free, male nor female" (Gal. 3:28; Col. 3:11). All are one in the eyes of God and in the eyes of the gospel. It is out of the question that some are better than others. All must come in exactly the same way, in humility. All are saved to serve God in the same way, with total commitment to him and others no matter who they are.

Outline
1. Salutation and thanksgiving *1:1-7*
2. Paul's appeal for Onesimus *1:8-21*
3. Concluding greetings *1:22-25*

Hebrews

Author: unknown, possibly Paul or
          Apollos
Date: between A.D. 60 & A.D. 70

Content

The key event in the last half of the first
century as far as the church was concerned
was the destruction of Jerusalem in A.D. 70. It
had been predicted by Jesus, and when it
happened, it marked the end of Christianity's
dependence on Judaism and the old order of
things. Not that Christians did not recognize
their Jewish heritage. They kept the Old Testament, modeled their worship after the syn-
agogue, worshiped the God of Israel, thought
of themselves as the fulfillment of prophecy,
acknowledged Jesus as the Messiah, and
described themselves as the inheritors of the
"new covenant" promised to Israel. But nonetheless they realized that the old order was
over. The end of the age had arrived. They
could experience the power of the new age in
the present through the salvation offered by
Christ. They also recognized that divisions of
race did not matter anymore; all are free to
come to Christ exactly the same way, by faith
in Jesus, God's Son.

To some of the Jewish believers this
created a problem. Their Jewishness meant
more to them than it should have, and they
were tempted to revert to the old order, aban-

doning their newfound faith in Christ. They wanted things to be as they had always been. But that could never be. The city of Jerusalem was gone, the temple destroyed, the priesthood disbanded. The nation was in shambles. The writer to the Hebrews was trying to point out that it is impossible to turn the clock back. We must press on in the new plan of God because the future is our goal, not the dead past.

It is not clear who wrote this book. Numerous people have been suggested, including Paul, Apollos, and Priscilla. After studying the problem, the church father Origen said that only God knows who wrote the letter to the Hebrews. It doesn't really matter. Whoever wrote it understood the situation well and was dealing with an important problem.

Theological Themes

Several themes can be found in this book. First, there is an emphasis on the superiority of Christ. To those Jewish believers who were wavering in their faith, the writer wanted to point out that there is nowhere else to go. Where can one find anything better than Jesus, who is the express image of God, better than Moses, better than Aaron, better than angels, better than anything? Jesus the Messiah is what they need.

Second, the obsolete nature of the old covenant and the establishment of the new covenant is stressed. The old is gone and the new has come. How could anyone want to go back to what God did not plan to keep? The old order served its purpose, and served it well, but its time is over. Now people are to come to Christ wherever they are, not by way of "Jerusalem"—except perhaps in a figurative way, through the heavenly Jerusalem.

Third, the writer speaks of the present glorious priesthood of Jesus in contrast to the defunct priesthood of Jerusalem. Jesus is now at the right hand of God eternally pleading our case. He knows what it is like to be human, so he can plead with understanding. We may go boldly to the throne of grace, there to find help in time of need.

Fourth, the Book of Hebrews stresses the need for perseverance. It is easy to quit and fall in the wilderness like the fathers of old. That ought never to happen again, and won't, if God's people do not lose heart.

Fifth, the writer extols the glories of faith and those who have exercised it. Chapter 11 is a marvelous sermon on those who endured, strengthened by their faith in the living God.

Finally, instructions for practical Christian living are given in chapters 12 and 13.

All of this together presents a complete defense of the Christian faith against its detractors and those who would look for salvation elsewhere.

Outline

James

Author: James
Date: c. A.D. 45-48

Content

The Book of James was written by the half-brother of Jesus. Evidently James had been unsure about the claims of Jesus during Jesus' lifetime, but following his resurrection became one of his most ardent followers. James was elected ruler of the church in Jerusalem and was well-liked by all, even the Jews who were opponents of Christianity. According to tradition, he had the nickname "the camel-kneed," because of the callouses on his knees from time spent in prayer. This was deeply respected by the Jews of antiquity as a sign of reverence and spirituality.

James wrote in a style reminiscent of Jesus and the Sermon on the Mount. Similarities can be found in about a dozen places, as well as other hints that what Jesus said was in the back of James's mind. The book is practical, straightforward, forceful, aimed at correcting errors, and without compromise. To read it is to be stricken in conscience because many of the problems addressed by James still exist in the church today. In essence the book is in the "wisdom tradition" that goes back to the Old Testament, in particular the Book of Proverbs. Over 50 commandments are given in this short homily.

Theological Themes

James was comparing true and false spirituality, the former called by him "pure" religion (1:27). It must come from the heart, be filled with understanding, and will issue forth in positive action. True spirituality is a life of faith in action. To be a hearer of the word and not a doer is to deceive ourselves (1:22). We must couple our profession of faith with overt evidence that we are changed people. James spent a lot of time (chapter 2) dealing with this problem. It is easy to say we have faith; the true test of faith is not our words, but our works. If someone knocks on our door and asks for help, what do we do? If we say, "I wish you well" and shut him out, that is a sure sign of unbelief. If we offer him help, that is a sign of belief. Some people find this emphasis disturbing because it seems to oppose what Paul said; it seems to imply that we are saved by our good works. We need to remember that Paul, too, stressed that faith must work (Gal. 5:6), we must bear one another's burdens (Gal. 6:2), and God has foreordained that those who are saved by faith will walk in good works (Eph. 2:10). James, on the other hand, was well aware that "every good and perfect gift" comes from God and is not earned (1:16-17). Their views are not contradictory.

True spirituality knows how to keep its mouth shut. Another section deals with the effects of evil speech (chapter 3). Too many people want to be heard, even when their minds are empty or filled with jealousy and ambition. When such a person speaks, discord abounds. A storm of evil is unleashed, and the suffering that results is enormous. True wisdom is good, peaceable, and meek (3:13). Just as Jesus was wise among us, a servant of all, so must we be wise in good works, decency, and humility.

True spirituality is unselfish, generous, impartial, and patient. All of this is emphasized in 4:1–5:7. We are not to look out for ourselves alone, but must learn what it means to love in deed as well as in theory.

Finally, true spirituality looks to God in prayer in all the events of life. God is able to help, and he values prayer. Prayer is always heard, and his answer is always the right one, no matter what it is, because he knows best.

Outline
1. Nature of true spirituality *1:1-27*
2. Relation of faith to works *2:1-26*
3. Bridling the tongue *3:1-18*
4. Practical exhortations *4:1–5:7*
5. Prayer and patience extolled *5:8-20*

Rulers Named in the New Testament

Ruler	Reference	Title	Relation to biblical narrative
Roman Empire			
Octavianus Augustus 31 B.C.-A.D. 14	Luke 2:1	Caesar	Ruled through the first half of Jesus' life.
Tiberius A.D. 14-37	Luke 3:1	Caesar	Ruled through the second half of Jesus' life.
Claudius A.D. 41-54	Acts 11:28; 18:2	Caesar	Ordered all Jews to leave Rome.
Nero A.D. 54-68	Acts 25:21-25; 27:1; 28:19	Caesar	Was the ruler Paul appealed to during his imprisonment by Felix and Festus. Beheaded Paul and crucified Peter.
Palestine			
Herod the Great 40 B.C.-4 B.C.	Matt. 2:1-22 Luke 1:5	King	Attempted to kill the baby Jesus by killing all the male children two years old or younger in Bethlehem.

Ruler	Reference	Title	Relation to biblical narrative
Archelaus 4 B.C.–A.D. 6*	Matt. 2:22	1st Procurator of Judea & Samaria	
Herod Antipas 4 B.C.–A.D. 39*	Matt. 14:1-10 Mark 6:14-28 Luke 3:1, 19; 9:7-9; 13:31; 23 Acts 4:27; 13:1	1st Tetrarch of Galilee & Perea	Beheaded John the Baptist. Pilate sent Jesus to Antipas for trial, but Jesus stood before him in silence.
Philip II 4 B.C.–A.D. 34*	Luke 3:1	1st Tetrarch of Iturea	
Pontius Pilate A.D. 26-36	Matt. 27:11-62 Mark 15 Luke 3:1; 13:1; 23 John 18-19 1 Tim. 6:13	6th Procurator of Judea & Samaria	Stood as judge at trial of Jesus.
Agrippa I A.D. 37-44	Acts 12	King	Beheaded the apostle James. Arrested Peter but he escaped with the help of an angel.

Ruler	Reference	Title	Relation to biblical narrative
Antonius Felix A.D. 52-58	Acts 23-24	12th Procurator of Judea & Samaria	Arrested and imprisoned Paul.
Porcius Festus A.D. 57-62	Acts 24:27; 25-26	13th Procurator of Judea & Samaria	As successor of Felix, Festus kept Paul a prisoner and finally sent him to Rome.
Agrippa II A.D. 52-70	Acts 25-26	4th Tetrarch of Galilee, Perea, & Iturea	Heard Paul's defense while Paul was imprisoned by Festus.

Key: *Caesar*—emperor of the Roman Empire; *Procurator*—the governor of a territory (e.g. Judea) not having the status of a province; *Tetrarch*—the ruler of a province (originally the province being 1/4 of the whole);

*When Herod died in 4 B.C. Palestine was divided among three of Herod's sons by Augustus.

1 Peter

Author: Peter
Date: c. A.D. 64

Content

Along with Paul, Peter was a leading figure in
early church history. Peter was among the first
converts to Jesus, leaving his home to travel
to the Jordan River while John the Baptist was
still preaching. He returned to his home on the
sea of Galilee, there to await Jesus' call to
active ministry. He was with Jesus during his
entire three years of preaching and became
one of the leading apostles, along with James
and John. When the three are listed in the
Gospels, Peter is always listed first, because
of his preeminence in the group. He was
singled out by Jesus as one who would be
foundational to the church (Matt. 16:16-19).
The church, *in fact*, is founded on Christ
(1 Cor. 3:11). But it was Peter who preached
on Pentecost, was instrumental in the spread
of the gospel, opened the door to the Gentiles
with his witness to Cornelius, and gave strong
support from the beginning. Peter was clearly
a rock on which the growth of the church
depended. Peter was not always a rock, however, and his denial of the Lord at his
crucifixion and his altercation with Paul (Gal.
2:11-14) show that his zeal could run hot and
cold. After Jesus' death and resurrection, Peter
exercised his ministry in Jerusalem, was then

forced to travel, and ended up in Rome where he was martyred during the reign of Nero, sometime between A.D. 64 and A.D. 68. Peter probably wrote this letter during those difficult days.

Theological Themes

Several themes run through the Book of 1 Peter. First, Peter wanted his readers to reflect on the greatness of salvation. We have an inheritance reserved in heaven for us. It is unfading, unchanging, and protected by God. If we are asked to give up our earthly lives, it does not matter by comparison with the glory that will be ours. If we are not asked to die for our faith, it is worth living for.

Second, Peter emphasized the need for spiritual growth. When we become believers we are like infants in need of simple nourishment. As we grow, we need more substantial food. Believers grow by nourishing themselves on prayer, meditation, reading God's Word, and fellowship. It would be great if we could all attain instant perfection, but such is not to be. Growth means effort, time, and patience.

Third, Peter spent a great deal of time talking about living the Christian life. We must realize that our time on earth is short; our lives are like grass that withers away. In light of that, we must stand firm against evil and refuse to conform to the destructive patterns of the age in which we live. It is so easy to become like everybody else, but we must resist that temptation. When persecutions arise, we must be ready to suffer, just as Jesus did. He left an example for us to follow (2:21-25). When Satan attacks we must resist him in faith, knowing that if we reject his offer he will depart from us (5:8-9). We must cast all our care and anxiety on the One who cares for us.

Fourth, Peter included specific instructions to husbands, wives, servants, and believers as citizens. His words revolve around commitment in love to one another, with a view to making life better for all. Finally, Peter singled out the leaders for admonition. Those who have oversight should realize that they are under the authority of God. No one should lord it over someone else; we are all under God. We are all to be clothed with humility, because God resists the proud and gives grace to the humble.

Outline
1. The nature of our salvation   *1:1-21*
2. Growth as a Christian   *1:22–2:10*
3. Instructions for Christian living   *2:11–3:22*
4. Ethical exhortations   *4:1-19*
5. Admonitions to church leaders   *5:1-14*

2 Peter

Author: Peter
Date: c. A.D. 64

Content

Peter wrote his second letter to the church at
large rather than to the specific churches in
upper Asia Minor. Some theologians dispute
that Peter actually wrote this letter, but there
are no compelling reasons to doubt that he was
actually the author.

Theological Themes

This short book has three basic themes. First,
Peter wanted to encourage the believers in
their Christian life. God's divine power has
provided us with all that we need to live for
him, but it remains up to us to make use of that
power. Peter said that we actually "participate
in the divine nature" (1:4). This probably
means roughly what Paul meant when he
spoke about Christians being the body of
Christ and united to him. The concrete way
that we make use of God's power is by exercise of spiritual virtues: faith, virtue, knowledge, self-control, steadfastness, godliness,
brotherly affection, and love. When these are
found in our lives we may have assurance that
our calling and election are real.

A second theme in this book is a description
of those who reject the gospel. They are

depicted in a long series of statements that are none too flattering (2:1-22). Peter is probably using a bit of polemical material that was more or less traditional at that time, because it reappears in the Book of Jude in much the same form.

A third theme concerns the second coming of Christ. Some were beginning to grow weary in waiting and were being taunted by those who disbelieved. Peter wanted to reassure his friends that Jesus is indeed coming back, at which time this world order will be renovated. The old order will dissolve and be replaced by a new heaven and new earth in which righteousness dwells.

Outline
1. Living the Christian life *1:1-21*
2. The nature of ungodliness *2:1-22*
3. The sure return of Jesus Christ *3:1-18*

1, 2, 3 John
Author: John
Date: c. A.D. 90-95

Content

These three letters are best taken together
because they were written at the same time to
the same church by the same author, the
apostle John. John had been an early follower
of Jesus, even during the days of John the
Baptist. He was a fisherman and had a volatile
temperament, with the nickname "son of
thunder." He was deeply attached to the Christian movement and became one of the dis-
ciples in the inner circle, along with Peter and
James. At the crucifixion, Jesus asked John to
take care of his mother Mary, indicating the
confidence that Jesus had in him. John wrote
the marvelous life of Jesus, or Gospel, that is
the fourth book of the New Testament. As-
sociation with Jesus changed John's temperament from being overly aggressive and loud
to being serene and loving. He lived in
Ephesus for most of the rest of his life, but was
at one point exiled to the island of Patmos
where he received the visions written down in
the Book of Revelation.

Theological Themes

Toward the end of the first century, false
theories had arisen that needed combating, in

particular, one that denied that Jesus really was a human being. It is interesting to note that the first christological error (false teaching about Jesus) was not a denial that he was God, but that he was a man. In our day the opposite is the case. People have no problem seeing Jesus as human, but sometimes struggle with the idea that he could be God incarnate. John stressed that Jesus was indeed human. He was seen, touched, and heard. John himself knew Jesus intimately as a human being.

In his first letter, the longest of the three, John spent a lot of time discussing the need for Christian living and how that works out in practice. We are to recognize that we: need God's grace; are to keep his commandments; love other human beings; resist the allures of the world, the flesh, and the devil; refrain from sinning; and test out anyone's claims to truth. John emphasized the importance of love. God is love and those who know how to love rightly know God truly. True love is liberating and healing. God sent Jesus to earth to embody and exhibit that love, so that as we believe in him we may have a similar love as our assurance that God is ours.

John also wanted Christians to be aware of the dangers that lurk around us. So much is anti-Christian. If we are not aware of this we might be taken in by it. To know it is to resist the devil and his attempts to take control of our lives.

Finally, John wanted Christians to have confidence in God and his work in our lives. We are not to be overcome by doubt, despair, anxiety, or fear. God is in control and can be trusted. We may be certain of our eternal life because we are certain about God. That knowledge should allow us to live freely and with strength in the face of opposition.

The second letter of John is written to an unnamed person called "the chosen lady." John said basically two things to her. First, he emphasized the need for love in the Christian life. Without love we do not know God. Second, he stressed the need for correct doctrine and the necessity to be on guard against those who reject the truth.

John's third letter is to an elder named Gaius. It is basically a practical exhortation to practice hospitality, follow the truth, imitate what is good, and stand against what is wrong.

Outlines

1 John
1. Living the Christian life   *1:1–2:2*
2. Living in fellowship with God   *2:3-29*
3. Living apart from sinfulness   *3:1-24*
4. Living in love   *4:1-21*
5. Living in confidence in God   *5:1-21*

2 John
1. Greetings   *1:1-3*

Jude

Author: Jude
Date: c. A.D. 64-70

Content

Jude, one of Jesus' half-brothers (Matt. 13:55), was considered the writer of this letter throughout most of the history of the church. Recently, doubts have been cast upon this, but there is no compelling reason to doubt his authorship.

Theological Themes

Three basic themes run through this short book. First, Jude wanted to warn believers against evil persons who were trying to use the gospel for their own ends. Those people found it easy to prey on the openness and sincerity of the believers, using them for immoral purposes. Jude warned Christians not to listen to everyone but to be certain when they committed themselves to anyone that that person was worthy of trust. Second, Jude wanted the believers to realize that they must take responsibility for the gospel and defend it when necessary. This does not mean that they are to go out of their way to be offensive, but when the necessity arises they are able to state with knowledge and conviction what they believe. If they do not do this, the wrong people will win out in the end. Finally, Jude gave a series of practical exhortations related to the Christian life. They are to build themselves up in the faith; pray in the Holy Spirit; live in God's love; wait for the mercy of Jesus to manifest itself; and refuse to take part in the immorality of their age. All this can be accomplished because Jesus is able to keep them from falling. He is our Lord and Savior, possessing divine glory, dominion, majesty, and authority, and able to protect us from all harm.

Outline

1. Greetings *1:1-2*
2. Defend the faith *1:3-4*
3. The evil detractors of the gospel *1:5-16*
4. Practical instructions *1:17-25*

REVELATION

Revelation
Author: John
Date: c. A.D. 95

Content

The Book of Revelation consists of seven
letters written by John the apostle to churches
in Asia Minor, along with a complex series of
visions that deal with world history, cosmic
struggle, and the end of the age. It is the most
difficult book in the Bible to understand, and
varied interpretations abound. In general,
there are four points of view: one sees the book
as dealing with John's day only (preterist);
another sees it as dealing with the end of the
age only (futurist); a third, as referring to the
whole church age (historicist); and a fourth, as
depicting the triumph of good over evil (poetic
or mythological). There are also subvarieties
of these views and combinations of them.
Probably a combination is the best way to
understand the book.

After the seven letters at the beginning,
there follow the visions. John first sees a complex picture of God on his throne, surrounded
by elders, angels, creatures, the Lamb, and
violent noises. It is an awesome experience
that prepares John for a series of three sets of
visions consisting of seals of a scroll opened,
trumpets blown, and bowls of judgment

poured out. The seals represent war, slaughter, famine, death, martyrdom, and the end of the age. The trumpets represent various plagues, judgments, sufferings, war, and death, ending again with the end of the age. The bowls represent disease, plagues, judgments, demonic spirits, destruction, and general mayhem. Scattered through this set of three complex visions are interludes that deal with world government, spiritual struggle, heaven, worship, angels, and false religion. The book ends with a glorious picture of heaven, where all tears are wiped away and God is all in all.

Theological Themes

John wrote down these visions at the command of God. Believers needed encouragement in a time of great persecution. To show them God in heaven and the saints surrounding him was intended to strengthen them to endure so that they too might take their places there. It was also to prepare the church for what was to take place during its history and especially before the end of the age. Written in veiled terms, the way things will go is depicted. Revelation was also written to show the triumph of good over evil and the certainty of Satan's defeat. We should never forget that evil survives because we choose to let it rule over us. We must resist it on every hand, using the power that God gives us. Finally, the book was written to show how victory is won through the power of the slain Lamb of God who appears as a triumphant Lion devouring his foes.

The principle actor in the book is the figure of the Lamb, who is dead yet living, and also a Lion. It is hard to imagine how all this appeared to John throughout the course of his visions, but that is how he describes it. He has only human words to picture what was an ineffable experience. As slain, the Lamb receives honor, glory, and blessing because his blood cleanses Christians from their sins. He, the light of heaven, prepares a banquet for those who have believed in him and endured sufferings in his name. He sits on the throne of heaven, sharing the glory of God forever. As Lion, the Lamb defends his own with a rod of iron; he has authority to open the scroll holding the wrath of God. He himself pours out wrath on those who have persecuted Christians. He defeats Satan and his forces, establishing righteousness forever.

The end of the book is a high note of comfort and encouragement. After darkness comes dawn; after suffering comes peace; after labor comes rest; after tears comes joy forevermore. It is marvelous to realize that life has meaning and is worth it. That realization gives us courage to carry on, no matter what.

Outline
1. Seven letters   *1:1–3:22*

New Testament Authors

Name	Nationality	Occupation	Writings	How he died
Matthew	Jew	tax collector	Gospel of Matthew	Tradition: died a martyr's death in Ethiopia
Mark	Jew		Gospel of Mark	Tradition: died a martyr's death
Luke	Greek	physician	Gospel of Luke	Tradition: died a martyr's death in Greece
			Acts of the Apostles	
John	Jew	fisherman	Gospel of John	Banished to Patmos A.D. 95 then released
			1, 2, 3 John	Tradition: died a natural death
			Revelation	
Paul	Jew	Pharisee/tentmaker	Romans	Tradition: beheaded at Rome on Nero's order A.D. 67 or 68
			1 & 2 Corinthians	
			Galatians	
			Ephesians	
			Philippians	